Teed Off

The Modern Guide To Golf

Double Eagle Press

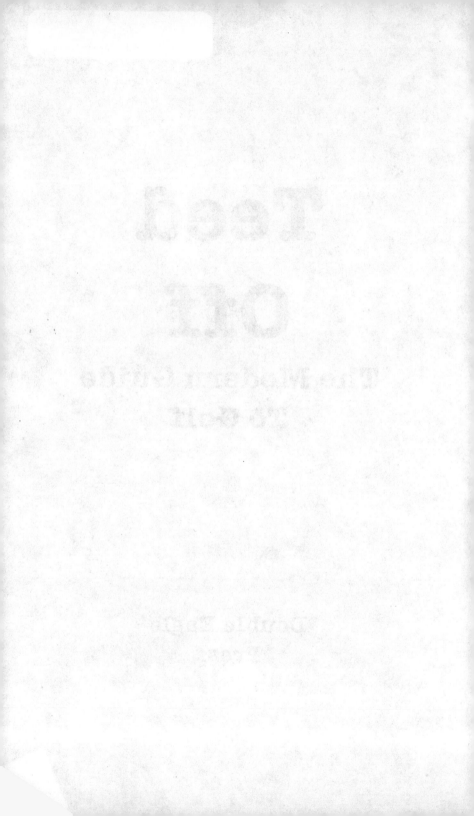

Teed Off

Off

The Modern Guide To Golf

Written & Illustrated

by

Tom Carey

First published March 13, 1995

Manufactured in the United States of America
ISBN: 1-877590-92-4

Published by
Double Eagle Press
1247 W. Wellington
Chicago, IL 60657

For my Dad,
who taught me everything I know about golf,
and a good deal of what
I know about life, too.

Thanks, Chop.

Contents

1. A HISTORY OF THE GAME
How Did It Begin &
Is It Too Late To Stop It Now?   9

2. EQUIPMENT
Are Fuzzy Alligator Head Covers
Really Necessary?   16

3. PLAYING THE GAME
People Pay Money To Do This?   33

**4. HOW DO YOU GET TO
PEBBLE BEACH?**
Practice   53

5. PROFESSIONAL GOLF
People Get Paid Money To Do This?   61

6. GOLFSPEAK
A Glossary Of Terms, Definitions
& Swearwords   81

**7. THE TEN COMMANDMENTS
OF MODERN GOLF**   97

GOLF:
Harmless Game Or Evil Curse?

Golf is a mysterious thing. Its history is shrouded in legend and lore. It is rich in arcane rules and customs, a pastime of gentlemen and ladies of breeding for over 100 years. It is a test of skill, of nerve and of imagination.

It is a test of skill when you must fade a little six-iron to a pin tucked behind a bunker. It is a test of nerve when you need to drain a side-hill five-footer to save par. And it is a test of imagination when you've got to explain to the wife why the new set of perimeter weighted irons you got was more important than the car payment.

Golf has evolved a lot in the last 100 years. Equipment has changed, rules have changed and hardly anyone wears a kilt anymore.

This book was written to help today's Golfer become a Golfer unbound by ancient rules and old traditions. A Golfer unafraid to wipe the beer from his face, tee it up with his naked lady tee, swing from the heels and watch proudly as his mighty clout sails into the great beyond.

A Golfer unafraid then to take a mulligan.

1.

A History Of The Game

How Did It Begin & Is It Too Late To Stop It Now?

THE MORRISES:
Young Tom, Olde Tom &
Other Dopey Names

Golf was invented one typically dark, rainy afternoon in St. Andrews, Scotland by Olde Tom Morris and his son, Young Tom Morris. (Scots are notoriously unimaginative about naming their kids.) They were sitting by the Loch Ness with their cameras waiting for the monster, when Young Tom absentmindedly took a swipe at a stone on the beach with his walking stick.

As fate would have it, the stone flew straight at an oak tree some yards away. As they walked up to the tree Olde Tom said, "I'll bet ye five bob ye kin nawt strike the tree wi' another stroke."

Though the rock lay just three feet from the tree, Young Tom began to shake and sweat from the pressure of the wager and he missed the putt. Furious, he smashed his stick against the tree and screamed, "It's the devil's oon game we've invented and I'll ne'er play it agin!"

Of course, he bought a new stick and was whacking stones on the beach again the next day. Which is how Young Tom Morris invented the yips and Olde Tom Morris invented the Nassau.

Young Tom Morris Invents Golf

GOLF IN AMERICA:
The Plague Spreads

For years the Morrises had the game of Golf to themselves. Then one sunny afternoon as they trudged along the beach looking for a lost ball, they came upon a family of vacationing Americans. Otto Bunker, a tailor, and his seamstress wife Anita, were sunbathing in the middle of the sixth green. The Scotsmen were livid.

"You kin naye lay aboot here, ya stupid gits!" cried Young Tom. "This is a Gahf links!"

Otto looked at the enraged Scotsmen in their plaid kilts and asked them to pose for a photo.

"The folks back home will love a shot of you fellas in those skirts," he said.

As Mrs. Bunker snapped the picture, Young Tom brained the tailor with his club, thereafter called a Cleek for the sound that it made on Otto's skull. The Bunker's attorney later used the photograph to win them a large cash settlement and the U.S. rights to the game of Golf.

Poor Young Tom Morris was plagued thereafter by nightmares in which chubby, pale Americans in bathing suits lay down in his line every time he tried to line up a putt.

Young Tom Morris Discovers The "Yips"

THE BUNKERS:
The First Family of U.S. Golf

So Otto and Anita came home the proud owners of two sets of golf clubs, several dozen balls and the right to build golf courses in the USA.

The Bunkers had plenty of time for their new hobby because although they were both expert clothiers, each was unutterably colorblind. Unscrupulous wholesalers had for years unloaded all their ugliest material on the unsuspecting Bunkers, who were able to sell nary a stitch of the awful clothing they made.

One day, in an effort to drum up business, Otto placed a newspaper ad offering a free round of Golf to anyone who bought a pair of trousers.

A couple of adventurous folks gave the new game, and the pants, a try, and in no time they were hooked. Before long every tailor for miles had built a golf course and the countryside was crawling with scores of Golfers, bashing their new golf balls, swinging their new golf clubs and buying pair after pair of the ugliest, loudest, tackiest, most horrible pants ever seen in North America.

Golf, as we know it today, was born.

Otto Bunker,
Founder of American Golf

2.

Equipment

Are Fuzzy Alligator Head Covers Really Necessary?

THE BALLS
Have You Got 'Em?

The first real golf balls were developed because the Morrises got fed up with breaking their expensive walking sticks on rocks. Just as the beaches of Scotland were about to disappear forever under piles of broken walking sticks, the Morris boys invented the "Featherie".

One day Young Tom, while cooking a goose for dinner, found that goose feathers shrunk considerably when boiled. He stuffed some inside a cover of stitched leather and when they dried they expanded to form a tight little golf ball.

Production of the "Featherie" was very slow until Tom's mom, Olde Lady Morris, suggested that he remove the goose feathers *before* boiling them. This spurred the growth of the new ball and saved many golf ball makers from having their eyes pecked out by enraged boiling geese.

The "Featherie" era lasted until about 1900 when a material called "Gutta Percha" was discovered in the Far East by bird lovers concerned about the fast disappearing goose population.

It was cheap, and it flew farther and lasted longer than the "Featherie". Soon golfers every-

The "Featherie"

where had switched to the "Guttie".

Sporting goods companies quickly realized that a serious Golf enthusiast would sell his children for five more yards on his tee ball.

The ensuing decades saw the rise and fall of balls made of rubber (the "Mooshie"), plastic (the "Gooshie"), and with centers made of cork (the "Corkie"), steel (the "Steelie"), glycerine (the "Mooshie-Gooshie") and even water (the "Jim Bob").

In the 60s, manufacturers settled on the two styles of balls we have today, thus beginning the "Modern Era" of golf balls and ending the "Stupid Nickname Era".

The goose population, meanwhile, has increased a thousand-fold due to the extinction of their chief predator, Scottish golf ball makers. The trauma inflicted upon their ancestors has not been forgotten by subsequent generations of geese who now flock to golf courses everywhere to "fertilize" the fairways, clog the water hazards and generally make life miserable for golfers.

Some relief may be in sight, however. The "Save The Geese Act of 1896" was recently repealed after several Senators had some very expensive shoes ruined at a celebrity pro-am. This will make it legal once again to boil geese alive.

THE CLUBS:
$1000 Graphite Garden Tools

Early clubs had names like the Moody, the Geek, the Panghorne and the Slap-Doodle. If you think it's hard to hit a 1-iron, you should try hitting a Slap-Doodle. The shafts of these clubs were wood and they made a satisfying snap when broken over the knee or heaved against a tree.

Unfortunately, they also often broke during the swing, which could be very disconcerting for the other players in the group. Many golfers were tragically killed by the flying remnants of shattered wooden shafts, a P.R. problem that threatened the popularity of the new game. It was very dangerous to play golf at this time.

The newly formed USGA solved this dilemma and rules problem, by allowing a free drop, two club lengths away from dead or injured players. And by allowing the manufacture of steel shafts.

Today, golf clubs are made from materials like graphite, magnesium and cadmium borite ascorbic acid. They allow the average player to hit it deep into the rough and to reach previously unreachable hazards.

And some can pick up police-band radio.

BY THE NUMBERS

The Driver

The Driver is a club used to tee off. It produces a high, short, soft shot, especially on holes with a water hazard in front of the tee.

The Fairway Woods

The Fairway Woods are the more lofted clubs that a player uses when he has hit his tee shot but is still a long way from the green. For most players that will be several times a hole. Many players find that these are easier to hit than long irons and so carry nothing but woods in their bags. This has led to the invention of such ridiculous clubs as the Wedge wood and the 27 wood.

The Irons

Irons are traditionally numbered 1 through 9 (since the end of the "Stupid Nickname" Era, anyway). Each one is a bit longer and less lofted than the club numerically following and is designed to go about 10 yards further. It is vitally important to know exactly how far you hit each club so you know how enraged to get when you leave an approach shot short, buried in a bunker.

The One Iron

This club is very difficult to hit. There is a famous golf joke which has Lee Trevino walking off a golf course in the rain holding a one-iron over his head to protect himself from lightning. "Even God can't hit a one-iron," says Lee, according to this gag. You will hear this joke every time you enter a golf club locker room. Which is one good reason to change your shoes in the parking lot.

The Pitching Wedge

The Pitching Wedge is a very lofted club used primarily around the green. It is used to launch a low, knuckling, line-drive type of shot.

The Sand Wedge

The Sand Wedge will produce the same kind of shot, even out of a bunker!

The Putter

The Putter is used to roll the ball along the ground. It is a very important club because most players will use it three or four times on each hole. This is the favorite club of many golfers and some have been known to keep dozens, or hundreds, stashed away in their basements.

Hitting The "Wedge"

GET A GRIP!
The Golf Glove

The golf glove is a very important piece of equipment that no golfer should be without. Hand sewn from the skin of goat embryos (I'm not making that up - I could never invent something that gross), the golf glove keeps the modern golfer's delicate hand from getting blisters and provides for a powerful grip. It also keeps your left hand pale and white while your right hand gets a dark tan which lets everyone you meet know that you are a proud and well appointed golfer. Or a Michael Jackson impersonator.

One should only remove a golf glove for putting or drinking beer. The latter is especially important because when it's really hot and your beer can gets all sweaty it could cause your golf glove to get wet and slippery. This, in turn, can cause the club to fly out of your hand during a swing and possibly injure the girl who drives the beer cart, thus depriving you of beer for the rest of the round.

So remember to always remove your golf glove when drinking beer.

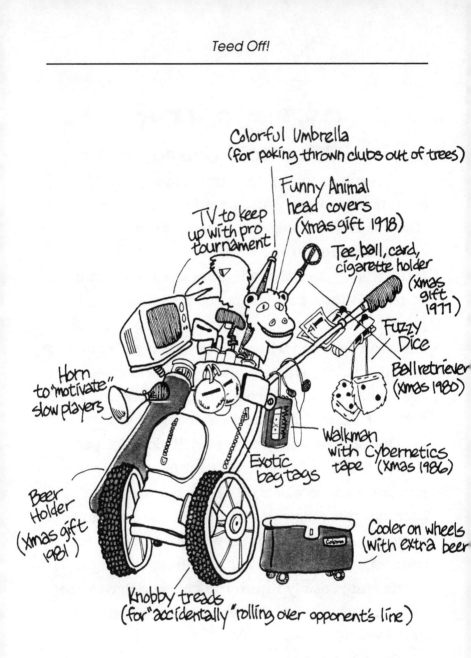

The Pull Cart

THE BAG:
If You Can Carry It Yourself, It's Too Small

Just as a woman needs a handbag to fit every occasion, a golfer needs a golf bag to do the same. (Feel free to use this analogy when you have to explain to the wife how you really needed that new eelskin job with the fur lined pockets.)

THE PULL CART

This is the traditional method of golf club transport. It has the convenience of an electric cart (i.e., wheels) yet still allows you to say that you are "getting some exercise." As though a five mile walk in six hours could be considered exercise. As a calorie burner, golf ranks right behind gin rummy.

The nice thing about a pull cart is that there is plenty of room on it for all the gizmos you will be receiving for birthdays and Christmas for the rest of your life. Grateful that they no longer need to spend time finding the perfect gift, family members will deluge you with plastic beer can holders, naked lady tees, exploding balls and fuzzy-faced animal-head head covers.

The Sunday Bag

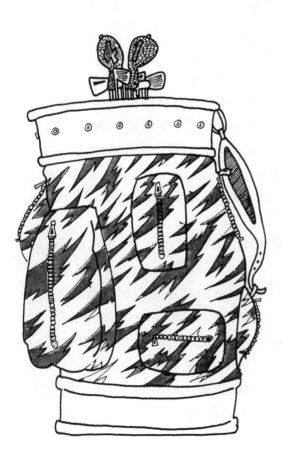

The Country Club Bag

THE SUNDAY BAG

The Sunday Bag is a small, lightweight bag about the size of your son's Ren & Stimpy back-pack. It is designed to hold a couple of clubs, a few balls and it folds up to fit in your glove box. This is important for those times when you're between sales calls and want to sneak in a few holes before lunch.

You can then sling the Sunday Bag over your shoulder and climb the fence of the nearby muni and play a few without paying. And run quickly with this lightweight bag on your back should the ranger chase after you in his electric cart.

THE COUNTRY CLUB BAG

You'll know you've really made it in the world of golf when you proudly purchase a golf bag that costs more than you paid for your first house. The Country Club Bag is more than a receptacle for your clubs, balls, sweaters, band-aids, socks, instruction manuals, gloves, visors, rainsuit, umbrella, shaving kit, rulebook and tape measure. Much more. It is a statement. It says "I have money." It says "I love golf." But mostly, it says "I pay someone else to carry my clubs."

truss
(for unlucky caddy)

rain suit, permanently wrinkled (Father's Day 1974)

pencil (broken lead)

USGA rules regulations 1969

rule book (xmas 1969)

personalized "Oh Shit" ball markers (xmas 1977)

tape measure (for closest to the pin arguments)

scorecard from the time you almost broke 100

two range balls (for water holes)

bag of personalized naked lady tees (xmas gift 1979)

Inside The Golf Bag

3.

Playing
The Game
If You Still Must

Letting Out The Shaft

DRIVING:
Getting Really Teed Off

In the beginning there is the Drive. There is nothing more satisfying than the sound and feel of a well-struck tee shot. Most of you, I know, will simply have to take my word for that.

The tee is a plot of ground where a player may place his ball on a peg called, surprisingly enough, a tee. This allows the player to sweep his club under the ball like a magician pulling a tablecloth out from under a pitcher of water.

The idea, on the tee, is for the player to take the biggest, longest, most unwieldy club in his bag, the Driver, and have a really wild swipe at the ball. Even if his tee shot flies deep into the woods or far out of bounds he will have released from inside all the rage and aggression that has built up since he missed that short par putt on the previous hole.

Once this pressure has been released he can chase down his errant shot in relatively good spirits. Players who spend a lot of time on the tee futzing around with trivialities, like aiming for instance, end up safely in the fairway a lot, which defeats the spirit and purpose of the game.

In The Fairway

FAIRWAY SHOTS:
A Very Short Chapter

Occasionally, even a player who swings so hard on the tee that he actually screws himself into the ground will hit his tee ball into the fairway. It happens so infrequently, however, that to go into a detailed explanation of fairway play would be rather pointless.

The Water Hazard
Scotland, Circa 1871

HAZARDS OF GOLF:
Over The River & Through The Woods

There is a saying in golf that "Trees are 90% air." You'll always hear this when trying to decide whether to chip safely and sanely back into the fairway or whether to hit a low rising 195 yard pull-hook over a bush, under a branch and around a water hazard. You will hear this from your opponents because they are sportsmen and lovers of the game, like you, and they thrill to see someone pull off a glorious one-in-a-million trick shot to save par from a densely wooded jail. Also, they want your money.

Next time an opponent tries to tell you that trees are 90% air, tell him that humans are 90% water and you'd like to drive your car through him to get a wash.

WATER HAZARDS & SAND TRAPS

The Water Hazard has been a traditional graveyard for errant golf balls since the days when the Morrises and their pals were banging featheries into the Atlantic Ocean. St. Andrews is a "links" golf course - 9 holes straight out and 9

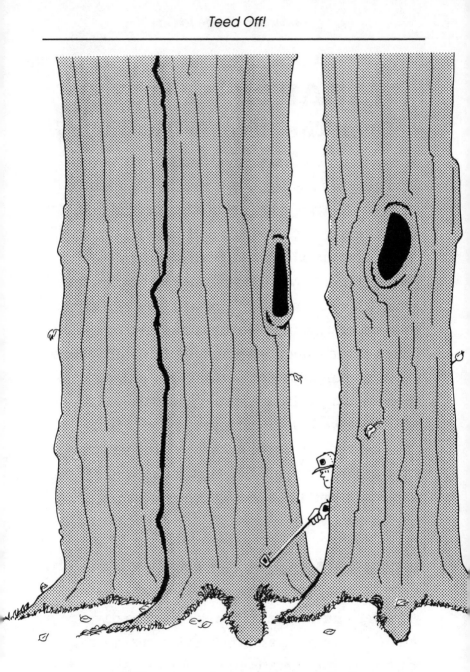

"Trees Are 90% Air"

holes straight back home - which means water on the left side of every hole on the front. This was a problem for Young Tom Morris since he hooked the ball wildly, while all the other players at the club faded the ball. For years he pounded balls into the briny deep while his partners chuckled and took his money.

One night, after a particularly difficult round, the angry young man took a shovel to the back nine of the course, determined to dig and dig until he struck water, thus equalizing the situation. Unfortunately, no matter where he dug, or how deep, all he found was sand.

Come morning, the first foursome on the links found Young Tom sprawled in one of the dozens of sand pits he had dug. He was fast asleep and having his recurring nightmare about the Bunker family, screaming out loud "Bunkers! The Bunkers are everywhere!"

Being Scotsmen, and too cheap to repair the damage, the rules committee convened and decided that the sand pits would stay and that from that day on all golf courses built would be required to have "Bunkers everywhere!"

The Sand Shot

THE SHORT GAME:
Chilly Dips & Fried Eggs

The Short Game is a term describing those crucial little shots around the green. For most golfers it is also a description of their tee shots, but let us not dwell on this.

THE CHIP SHOT

When a player is ten yards or closer to the green he must hit a chip shot. What makes a chip shot different from other ten yard shots is that it is only meant to go that far.

THE PITCH SHOT

The pitch shot is a high, soft shot which will stop quickly as it lands gently in a bunker in someone's footprint. Which leaves you with...

THE SAND SHOT

What to do when your ball is buried so deep in the sand that you need a permit from the gas company to play it? Any pro will tell you that sand shots are "easy" Use the Sand Wedge, a heavy, lofted club to inflict the maximum amount of pain on any pro who says this too often.

43

The "Over 40" Putter

PUTTING:
Yippy-Ay-Yay

Since the day Young Tom Morris yipped it at St. Andrews, golfers everywhere have sweated, twitched and gagged over the simple task of rolling a ball into a hole.

Golfers will try anything to improve their putting. When Sam Snead began squatting over his putts croquet-style in a vain attempt to cure his yips, millions of weekend hackers began squatting over their putts, too. The USGA quickly outlawed this practice for being "really stupid."

When Jack Nicklaus won the Masters with a putter as big as his own head, millions began toting 25 lb. "Nicklaus-Head" blades. These, too, were outlawed, but not before a startling number of players and caddies were felled by hernias.

The current trend among the "putting-impaired" is the extra-long putter. This club was first used by seniors whose arms had seemingly become too short to read restaurant menus, see their shoelaces clearly and make three footers. It makes the player look tremendously silly when hitting a putt, but then, most of them are already used to looking that way on a golf course.

Foul Weather Golf

BLOWIN' IN THE WIND:
Braving The Elements

Sooner or later, (sooner if you have a regular tee time reserved that you'd like to keep) you're going to get stuck playing in the rain. When faced with a fast-moving incoming storm my Dad used to say "Hell, son, you know it never rains on a golf course! Let's keep playing!" That was before he got hit by lightning while lining up a putt. If you think South Florida was a disaster area after Hurricane Andrew, you should see my old man's putting stroke these days.

Any player who's really serious about golf will learn to play wearing boots, ski gloves, hand warmers, polypropylene long-johns, three sweaters, two jackets, a scarf and earmuffs. This can actually be a blessing. When you find yourself too bound up to take a swing that remotely resembles something golf-like and your tee ball veers wildly and strikes the only other person loony enough to be on a golf course that day, you'll be too wrapped up in extra clothing to be recognizable, thus avoiding potentially costly litigation.

KEEPING SCORE:
The Foot Wedge & Pencil Iron

Keeping a golf score can be complicated. Like much in this world, it is open to interpretation. Oh, there are purists who insist that all putts be holed and all shots counted, but as Al Capone used to say, "Everything's negotiable, right?"

When you flog your ball into a waste area and take several brutish swipes at it before it comes out, jarring loose a bush, three rocks and a robin's nest in the process, you may want to estimate your final total. "I *think* I had a 7," you'll say, when asked. By feigning memory loss you, like others who have pled insanity in L.A. courtrooms, have effectively thrown yourself upon the mercy of your peers, who know that they, too, may have an attack of "Golfer's Amnesia" before the round is over and so will likely not complain.

Also, when reporting your final score it is important to add a short addendum. You didn't have a "94". You had a "94-with-two-out-of-bounds-on-13-and-three-three-putts on the front." As if it were the cruel fates that caused your drives to fly into that condo owner's bowl of Rice Chex and not your own wicked slice.

WHERE TO PLAY:
A Course Is A Course,
Of Course, Of Course

The Public Course is where most folks get their first taste of the wondrous game of Golf. Most are run by benevolent fellows who love the game and want to bring it to the greatest number of people. And because local zoning laws won't let them plow the place under and put up a mall.

The most coveted prize in Golf isn't the Ryder Cup or the Masters trophy. It's the Permanent Tee Time. Win one and you'll play every Saturday at 5AM (or 4:08 PM or midnight or whatever time they damn well say) from March to December. It doesn't matter if a tornado or a snowstorm hits or you suffer cardiac arrest. If you don't find a sub before they load you into the ambulance the Public Course will auction your place off to the highest bidder for more than it costs a Japanese businessman for a Van Gogh.

See, there are a million golf junkies just like you, hooked so bad that they'll actually pay money to shoot 147 on a course where the fairways are harder than an interstate expressway and the greens are bumpier than a teenager's face.

THE COUNTRY CLUB:
"The Six Iron, Jeeves"

There are some differences between playing golf at a crowded, low-quality Public Course and playing at an exclusive, well-manicured Country Club. About 50,000 differences, actually.

A Country Club is an organization of doctors, lawyers and men who have not yet squandered their large inheritances, who have gotten tired of waiting in the damp, frozen dawn for a tee time at some overplayed, worn out public golf course. These men write Harvard tuition-sized checks each year for the privilege of waiting in the damp frozen dawn for a tee time at their own private club. Plus they get free coffee and Danish.

But to a serious golfer the lure of the Country Club is much stronger than that. In addition to having a well-groomed course, there's the complimentary body talc in the shower, the freedom to tell sexist and racist jokes in the card room (especially important for judges and politicians) and a swell plastic bag tag with their club affiliation on it (so airline baggage handlers will look at their golf bag and say "Hey, this guy belongs to a country club. Let's rifle the pockets!")

4.
How Do You Get To Pebble Beach?

Practice

THE SWING:
Flying Elbows & Rusty Gates

No physical movement in the history of sport has been analyzed, dissected, diagrammed, studied and discussed more than the golf swing. Golf magazines devote hundreds of pages to controversial issues like head tilt and thumb placement. High speed photography, once used only in military research, has emerged as a whole new field in golf. The Army now lures young men into the service with the promise that after they're discharged they will be highly trained photographers ready to start a lucrative career shooting ten-frames-per-second photos of pro golfers for instructional articles.

In reality, the golf swing is not that complex. Just keep your head down, keep your eye on the ball, keep your left arm straight, keep your left foot at a 45 degree angle to the intended line of flight, keep your right elbow tucked in, keep the swing path inside-out, keep the club horizontal at the top of the backswing, shift your weight, delay your release, hit down and through the ball, don't peek, stay balanced and follow through to the target. It's just that easy!

The Swing

DE-RANGED:
On The Ol' Rock Pile

The driving range is an empty lot where golfers pay real, hard-earned, after-tax cash for the privilege of pounding rock-hard chunks of red striped ovoids into an empty field.

There are 16th century murals depicting the tortures of Hell that resemble nothing so much as the huddled masses gouging up the Astroturf mats at the local Stop-N-Sock.

The driving range proprietor will gleefully sell you a wire basket full of nicked and dented objects similar in appearance to golf balls. If the interstates were paved with the material from which these balls are made construction workers from coast-to-coast would be forced to find another place to sit in their trucks and eat doughnuts.

Periodically, a minimum-wage Generation-Xer in a hockey helmet will drive out in a souped up gas cart and tractor to scoop them up so that they may be hit again. And again. And again.

The range won't improve your game much, but dinging a few off the pick-up cart may help you develop a punch shot that you can use when you end up under one of those "90% air" trees.

The Driving Range

THE OFF-SEASON:
Rug Putting & Garage Golf

The truly dedicated golfer maintains a fierce and demanding practice schedule in the off-season. (The off-season being those few weeks when the average temperature is below ten degrees fahrenheit.)

Rather than risk losing his swing over a few month's rest, the dedicated player will set up his own in-home practice area. If you are lucky enough to live in a home or apartment with high ceilings and shag carpeting you just need to hang netting over all the walls and you'll be ready to hit golf balls whenever and where ever the mood strikes.

If you don't have high ceilings (or if you're married) you'll have to use the garage for your practice area. Just pick up one of those huge nets you'll find advertised in the back of golf magazines next to the ads for balls that go 500 yards and the "Hypnotize Your Way To A Better Swing" videotapes. They only cost a few thousand bucks and are easy to assemble as long as you're a Japanese auto mechanic and have access to a variety of exotic power tools.

Rug Putting

Spend an hour a day in the off-season hitting balls into your net and by spring you'll have locked into muscle-memory at least twenty new and difficult-to-change swing habits. Your reflexes will get a workout , too, as you dodge the errant golf balls ricocheting around your garage.

Come spring you can dismantle the thing and toss it into that rusting metal shed you put up in the back yard where it can gather dust next to the weight bench, rowing machine and stationary bike that you also bought and now never use.

Keeping your short game in shape in the off-season is a much easier proposition. Simply shave down a chunk of carpeting in your home, say, the living room area, to the speed of a well-kept putting green. Then you can practice your putting all the time. If you pull up the carpeting and stuff objects under it (a dish, a glass, stacks of old magazines, the cat) you can create real bends and breaks, thereby customizing your little indoor putting surface.

Again, this is only for those of you who are not married. Or who wish to soon be not married.

5.

Professional Golf

People Get Paid To Do This?

PROS & CONS:
Do The Hustle

The early professional golfer was usually a former caddy who spent his formative years toting the bags of rich folks with bad pants and too much time on their hands and who was clever enough to notice a few things about them. One, they loved golf. Two, they bet big cash. Three, most of them couldn't make a par if you put them on the ladies' tee and gave them two mulligans.

The enterprising young caddy would quickly learn this game that rich folks found so difficult and, if he was enterprising enough, would play the rich folks and separate some of them from their cash. Often, after many humiliations, all the rich folks in the area would get together and agree to make a lump-sum monthly payment to the young man if he would just hang around and *not* play them. And so, the pro golfer was born.

Most settled into country club life, teaching golf lessons, overcharging members for shirts, hats and golf umbrellas, drinking at the clubhouse bar and carrying on torrid affairs with the bored wives of club members who spent every waking hour on the golf course.

Sooner or later, even the most nearsighted of rich guys would figure out what was going on and realize that something would have to be done about the club pro "problem."

As the rich businessmen traveled, meeting and talking with other rich businessmen, it became clear to them that this club pro/bored wife/ cheap golf shirt phenomenon was occurring all over the United States. The rich guys decided it was time to get the club pros out of town. They got together to sponsor tournaments in the South and West, far from their country clubs, and they sent their pros on the road. Whenever one threatened to quit and come home, the rich guys would raise the tournament prize money and the pros would stay just a little bit longer.

Thus the golf tour evolved as a way for rich guys to keep their troubled marriages intact and to keep themselves from being fleeced of their fortunes by professional golf hustlers.

Of course, as soon as the pros were out of their hair, they went back to the golf course with a vengeance, leaving their golf-widowed wives as bored as ever. Which leads me to the story of how the professional tennis tour began...but, that's another book, isn't it?.

The Teaching Pro

THE TOURING PRO:
Money For Nuthin', Sticks For Free

Professional golfers today have little in common with the original tour playing hustlers. These days, each pro is carefully manufactured in a golf professional factory in North Carolina. Each is tall, thin and blond and has a swing that is mechanically perfect. Everyone gets free clothes, free equipment, free cars and free houses, from the rich guys who own the companies that make these things and who are still afraid of being cuckolded by tan, good-looking golf pros.

The purses on the professional golf tour have gotten bigger and bigger so that, nowadays a professional golfer doesn't even have to win to make a living. Most of the time, he can stroll the fairways of some fabulous resort golf course, shoot around par, come in thirtieth and still make about 4 kazillion dollars a year.

(That's not counting endorsement money from company presidents who want him to stay away from their wives in the off-season, too.)

The Touring Pro

TOTALLY TUBULAR GOLF:
A TV Guide

Golf is a sport made for television. From the heart-racing sight of a middle-aged man in ugly pants strolling down the fairway to the incisive commentary of an announcer with a phony British accent describing how courageous it is to hit a 9-iron from the rough, the action never stops.

The British Announcer

Each telecast employs an announcer from England. Oftentimes one whose only qualification is that he has the kind of haughty, arrogant accent that makes Americans feel like their flies are unzipped. Networks hire these guys to lend an air of authenticity to a tournament, as though the "Greater-Tri-Cities-Tang-Simulated-Orange-Breakfast-Drink Open" were an historic event.

These Limeys make cute, Britishy comments like "Bad luck with the loosely bound upsy-down niblick-mashie from the dreadful heather." This might sound good to a TV exec, but real Americans change the channel when they hear something that sounds like a cricket match.

Golf On TV

The Mediocre Ex-Pro Announcers

These announcers are in the twilight years
of careers so bad that they are actually happier to
miss a cut than make one because their chances
of making money on TV are so much better than
if they were to try to finish the tournament.

They all speak in a lazy Southern drawl as
though they grew up in a Texas caddyshack in-
stead of an exclusive Northeastern country club
and haven't had to so much as carry their own
bag since they were twelve.

It's a good gig for these guys. They sit in a
tent watching TV monitors, swilling beer and jok-
ing about how bad they played in this week's
tournament and get paid for it. Pro golfers are
generally such boring human beings that if one
of these guys possesses even the faintest glimmer
of a personality he can make big bucks by being a
"Tell It Like It Is" sports journalist. And still play
well enough to get $10,000 a pop for those Mon-
day afternoon corporate outings.

The Roving Announcer

Recently, the TV folks have been sending one
Mediocre Ex-Pro Announcer out of the beer tent
and on to the golf course to get up close coverage

The Roving Announcer

of the players. The announcers decide who has to go by swilling beer until someone has to go to the Porta-Potty. Whoever gives up first loses.

The Roving Announcer gets close to the pro and asks important questions about strategy and grip pressure while the pro decides how in the hell he's going to play a ball that has come to rest on a half-eaten cheeseburger. This is exciting for viewers because they never can tell when the player will look straight into the camera and suggest loudly that the Roving Announcer has an illegal relationship with his mother.

"He's in absolute jail here, folks," he'll say, when he sees the ball glued to the Velveeta, "he's got *no* chance to get to the green. Why he'll probably roll over on his back and whine like a dog when he sees this lie. You know, if God and Arnold Palmer came in here with a Caterpillar tractor they couldn't get the ball out of this rough."

Then, when the pro lofts a shot between two trees and on to the green, the Roving Announcer will fall to his knees weeping and declare that the Pope and several Congressmen name the site a Holy Golf Shrine to which pilgrims could trek barefoot to see where Joe CorporateVisor made par to lock up the Cheez-Whiz Invitational.

THE MAJORS:
Masters Of The Universe

The Masters

The Masters Tournament was begun by the great Bobby Jones. He remained an amateur throughout his career because of his dedication to the spirit of sportsmanship, his belief in the purity of the game and because he believed professional golfers were the lowest kind of scum.

The Masters is run by a committee of the six remaining survivors of the battle of Gettysburg who have decreed that everything at the tournament be painted "Masters Green," from the refreshment stands to the Port-A-Potties. This can be very confusing and it's why you should be careful when buying a beer there.

Augusta National has wide fairways, no rough, few bunkers and no O.B. What makes it so difficult is the knowledge that if you accidentally wear an outfit that doesn't include the color "Masters Green" the rules committee will send a half-dozen members of the Daughters of the Confederacy around to bludgeon you about the head and neck with their parasols and force you to

The Masters

sing twenty choruses of Dixie.

The winner of the Masters is presented with the traditional "Green Jacket" by the year's previous winner. This is considered a great achievement and honor and each year, all the previous winners get together at a banquet in their green jackets and eat green food. Which is why nobody ever wins the Masters two years in a row.

The U.S Open

Qualifying for the U.S. Open begins each year in January and is open to everyone on the planet, whether they play golf or not. Local, county, state, regional and sectional qualifying rounds, which run for five months, reduce the field to the 4200 players who begin teeing off before dawn on the first day. After two rounds, the field is cut to those 67 over par or better (and ties) and those not hopelessly lost in the 11 foot deep rough.

The U.S. Open is administered by the USGA, an organization of high handicappers who feel that it should be less a test of golf and more a test of hunting for lost golf balls. They chuckle gleefully at the thought of the best players in the world teeing off with 7 irons and lagging from 6 feet to keep from shooting over 100.

The U.S. Open

The British Open

Early British Opens were always won by
either Olde Tom Morris or Young Tom Morris.
Mostly because nobody ever entered but Olde
Tom Morris and Young Tom Morris. Actually,
the Morris boys never actually told anybody what
the hell it was they were doing out there on the
beach which pretty much made the two of them a
lock for first and second place.

In the years after golf came to the U.S., the
British Open was almost always won by an American pro who would arrive two weeks early and
immerse himself in the culture to prepare for the
event. He would buy a tweed cap, drink warm
beer, eat mutton and learn to play the bump and
run. He would hire a colorful, 97 year-old local
caddy who smoked a briar pipe and said "Aye, yee
kin nae git ta thet grin wi' oot a wee bet more
shillelagh" when he meant "Hit more club."

In recent years, American pros have quit
playing the British Open in droves. They don't
wish to waste two valuable weeks of their careers
on history and tradition when they could be playing an exhibition round with executives from the
food additive industry. And who can blame
them? Warm beer and mutton. Ugh.

The British Open

The PGA

The last major tournament of the year is the PGA, for which every single professional golfer in the country is eligible - even the toothless 78 year-old guy who chases kids off the local miniature golf course. What usually happens at the PGA is that one of these obscure local pros shoots a 68 in the first round to lead the field.

After answering questions from curious sportswriters in the press tent, ("Who the hell are you?") the obscure club pro will be descended upon by major international corporations eager to be represented by such an inspiring "up-from-his-own-bootstraps" type of guy. By Friday's round the obscure club pro will have company names on his shirt, hat, bag, shoes, caddy and tattooed on all visible parts of his body.

Touring pros always love when this happens, and they'll offer the club pro help and advice. ("Boy, it's great the way you hit it so square with that funny hitch in your backswing!")

Unused to the pressure, and to the extra weight of the advertisements now sewn to his body, the obscure club pro inevitably shoots 90 and the PGA is eventually won buy the usual anonymous touring pro.

6.

GolfSpeak

A Glossary Of Terms, Definitions & Swearwords

Alligator   1. Animal native to Florida that lives in water hazards and preys on golfers trying to retrieve balls. 2. Animal native to expensive golf shirts.

Athlete's Foot   The only athletic part of a golfer.

Attitude Adjuster   Beer, or other adult beverage consumed for the purpose of improving one's outlook on the back nine.

Bag Tag   Plastic ornament attached to bag to indicate courses where player has played. Number of bag tags is generally in direct inverse proportion to ability.

Ball Washer   Device which promotes the efficient evaporation of water.

Barbeque   Something people who live next to golf courses never do.

82

Barbeque

Bogie   1. One over par. 2. Casablanca.

Break   1. Amount of "turn" in a putt,
                   as in "I think it breaks 6 inch-
                   es to the left." 2. What golfer
                   does to putter after said putt
                   breaks 6 inches right.

Breeze   Any wind under 50 mph, as in
                   "Let's not quit just because of
                   this little breeze!"

Casual Water   Any water in which your ball
                   lands.

Cup   1. Plastic liner in hole. 2. Con-
                   tainer for *Attitude Adjuster*.

Double Bogie   1. Two over par. 2. Casablanca,
                   The Maltese Falcon.

Duck   1. Migratory bird which inhab-
                   its water hazards and quacks
                   in golfer's backswings. 2.What
                   people who live next to golf
                   courses and still barbeque do.

Casual Water

Fade
1. A shot that curves slightly from left to right, favored by many pros. 2. What the average player does after playing the first four holes in 2 under.

Fence
1. Barrier separating golfers from irate homeowners. 2. Man who buys sets of golf clubs from frustrated players at ten cents on the dollar and later resells them for face value to the original owner.

Grip
1. Action of holding on to a golf club in a way that makes it nearly impossible to swing. 2. What a golfer loses after 3 putting from six feet.

Hacker
Any player in the group in front of you who plays slower than you think he should. (See *Maniac*.)

Fence

Halfway House   1. Place where golfers stop for rest and refreshment after the ninth hole. 2. Place where golfers who have been driven insane by the game and who have committed major felonies go to rehabilitate after serving out their prison terms.

Handicap   Statistical figure arrived at through a series of calculations indicating how much money a player thinks he can win from his opponents.

Head Cover   1. Knit or leather stocking designed to protect clubs. 2. Position golfer assumes upon hearing a cry of "fore."

Keeper   Any divot over six inches in length, suitable for "keeping" and planting in the backyard.

Lightning   God's way of telling you you've been playing too much golf.

Keeper

Links

1. Early golf courses, named for their unique, seaside configuration. 2. Style of chain fence designed so that golf balls can pass right through.

Locker Room

Area of club house where golfers can change their clothes and their scorecards.

Maniac

Any player in the group behind you playing faster than you would like. (See *Hacker.*)

Rough

1. Long grass on either side of the fairway where most tee shots land. 2. Surface of a club that has been dragged across the parking lot.

Sand Wedge

An iron designed to enable a golfer to move huge amounts of sand from directly beneath a golf ball without actually touching it.

Sand Wedge

Shank   1. A ball hit directly sideways
              2. The part of the club buried
              in the ground after this shot.

Snickers 1. Candy bar eaten at the half-
              way house. 2. Sound made by
              caddies watching your swing.

Sprinkler Watering device built into fair-
              ways designed to automatically
              spray the area whenever a
              player is within ten feet.

Stroke   1. Attempt to advance the ball
              with a swing. 2. Seizure
              brought on by attempts to ad-
              vance the ball with a swing.

Tee Marker Objects designating the teeing
              area set up at an angle which
              makes it impossible to hit a
              straight tee shot.

Tee Plant The act of driving a tee into the
              ground in the hopes that some-
              day a tee tree will grow there.

Sprinkler

Triple Bogie 1. Three over par. 2. Casablanca, The Maltese Falcon, The African Queen.

Wind Weather phenomenon created by a player who has too many beers and chili dogs at the halfway house.

Yardage 1. Measurement used by courses to estimate distance of holes, usually accurate. 2. Measurement used by players to estimate distance of shots, usually inaccurate.

Yips 1. Affliction that causes you to tremble, twitch and sweat profusely over short, important putts. 2. Sound your opponent makes when you miss a short, important putt.

Tee Plant

7.

The Ten Commandments Of Modern Golf

One
THOU SHALT NOT CARRY A BALL RETRIEVER

Any ball that goes in a hazard is gone! Do not hold up the whole course so you can search around in the muck for a couple of yellowed, waterlogged X-outs. If you can't afford to lose a ball or two you can't afford to play the game.

Two
THOU SHALT CARRY THY CLUBS IN A SUITABLE BAG

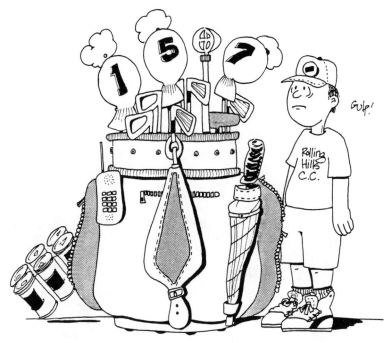

Your bag should house no less than 2 dozen balls, three sweaters, a rain suit, an umbrella, 8 old gloves, a swing-weight, 600 tees, a ball marker, spare spikes, 10 old scorecards, 5 broken pencils, a can of insect repellent, band-aids, a roll of toilet paper and a tuna sandwich.

Three

THOU SHALT NOT LET GROUPS "HIT UP" ON PAR THREES

"Hitting up" was begun by the early Scots to see how many people they could hit with their flying Featheries. This did thin out the number of players clogging up the courses, but otherwise it's a waste of time.

Four
THOU SHALT NOT USE THE WORD "GOLF" AS A VERB

You do not "golf". You "play golf". Players who use the word golf in this manner will be soundly paddled by the rules committee.

Five
THOU SHALT NOT WALK

Are you crazy? You could have a heart attack! Besides, you need a cart to put your beer cooler in.

Six

THOU SHALT NOT PLAY GOLF WITH THY SPOUSE

Unless you want a quick and nasty
divorce.

Seven
THOU SHALT NOT EXPLAIN THY ROUND IN EXCRUCIATING DETAIL

If you force someone to go all 18 holes with you they should get caddie fees.

Eight
THOU SHALT NOT STEP IN THY OPPONENTS LINE

Unless you're absolutely sure you can get
away with it.

Nine
THOU SHALT HONOR THY GOLF PRO

Hey, he's figured out how to make a living playing a game while you still can't break 100.

Ten
THOU SHALT KEEP HOLY
THE SABBATH

Never miss your Sunday tee time. I don't
know who built the church, but God made
the grass and the sunshine and that tree
you lie four behind. So enjoy.

Tom Carey is a writer/illustrator from
Chicago. His previously published
work includes
The Modern Guide To Sexual Etiquette,
and *The Marriage Dictionary* .

He has a 4 handicap and only breaks a
club if it really, really deserves it.

Also available from
Double Eagle Press:

The Marriage Dictionary	$ 6.95
The I Love To Fart Diet	$ 6.95
The Modern Guide To Sex, Too!	$ 7.95
Teed Off! A Modern Guide To Golf	$ 7.95
The Club Thrower's Handbook	$ 9.95
Your Baby: An Owner's Manual	$ 7.95
Baby's 40th Birthday Book	$10.95

Double Eagle Press
books are distributed through
Sourcebooks, Inc.
1-800-SBS-8866